First World War
and Army of Occupation
War Diary
France, Belgium and Germany

47 DIVISION
Divisional Troops
Divisional Cyclist Company
15 March 1915 - 31 July 1916

WO95/2717/2

The Naval & Military Press Ltd
www.nmarchive.com
Published in association with The National Archives

Published by

The Naval & Military Press Ltd

Unit 10 Ridgewood Industrial Park,

Uckfield, East Sussex,

TN22 5QE England

Tel: +44 (0) 1825 749494

www.naval-military-press.com

www.nmarchive.com

This diary has been reprinted in facsimile from the original. Any imperfections are inevitably reproduced and the quality may fall short of modern type and cartographic standards.

© Crown Copyright
Images reproduced by permission of The National Archives, London, England, 2015.

Contents

Document type	Place/Title	Date From	Date To
Heading	WO95/2717 March 1915-Jul 1916 Divisional Cyclist Co		
Heading	47th Division 47th Divl Cyclist Company Mar 1915-July 1916		
Heading	47th Division 47th Divl Mounted Troops Cyclist Coy Vol I 15.3.31.7.15		
War Diary	Redbourn	15/03/1915	15/03/1915
War Diary	Havre	16/03/1915	17/03/1915
War Diary	Arques	18/03/1915	19/03/1915
War Diary	Marles-Les-Mines	20/03/1915	17/04/1915
War Diary	Hurionville	18/04/1915	24/04/1915
War Diary	Bethune	25/04/1915	07/05/1915
War Diary	Beuvry	08/05/1915	09/05/1915
War Diary	Wood Between Beuvry and Le Quesnoy	10/05/1915	01/06/1915
War Diary	Vaudricourt	02/06/1915	08/06/1915
War Diary	Noeux-Les-Mines	09/06/1915	12/06/1915
War Diary	Hesdigneul	13/07/1915	14/07/1915
War Diary	Noeux-Les-Mines	15/07/1915	31/07/1915
Heading	47th Division 47th Cyclist Coy Vol II From 1st To 31st August 1915		
War Diary	Noeux-Les-Mines	01/08/1915	02/08/1915
War Diary	Bois Des Dames	03/08/1915	29/08/1915
War Diary	Noeux-Les Mines	30/08/1915	31/08/1915
Heading	47th Division 47th Divl Cyclist Coy Vol III Sept 15		
War Diary	Noeux-Les-Mines	01/09/1915	23/09/1915
War Diary	Houghin	24/09/1915	24/09/1915
War Diary	Field Near Mazingarbe	25/09/1915	26/09/1915
War Diary	Les Brebis	27/09/1915	30/09/1915
Heading	47th Division 47th Cyclist Coy Vol IV Oct 15		
War Diary	North Maroc	01/10/1915	02/10/1915
War Diary	Wood Near Gosnay	03/10/1915	04/10/1915
War Diary	Labeuvriere	05/10/1915	06/10/1915
War Diary	Noeux-Les-Mines	07/10/1915	24/10/1915
War Diary	Mazingarbe	25/10/1915	31/10/1915
Heading	Cyclist Co 47th Div Nov Vol V		
War Diary	Mazingarbe	02/11/1915	14/11/1915
War Diary	Hurionville	15/11/1915	30/11/1915
Heading	47th Cyclist Co Dec Vol VI		
War Diary	Hurionville	01/12/1915	01/12/1915
War Diary	Ligne	02/12/1915	02/12/1915
War Diary	Hurionville	03/12/1915	03/12/1915
War Diary	Noeux-Les-Mines	04/12/1915	23/12/1915
War Diary	Sailly-Labourse	24/12/1915	24/12/1915
War Diary	Lancashire Trench	25/12/1915	25/12/1915
War Diary	Northampton Trench	26/12/1915	28/12/1915
War Diary	Lancashire Trench	29/12/1915	30/12/1915
War Diary	D.2 Sector	31/12/1915	31/12/1915
Heading	Cyclist Coy 47 Div Jan Vol VII		
Heading	47 Cyclist Coy Vol VI		
War Diary	Sailly-Labourse	01/01/1916	02/01/1916

War Diary	Houchin	03/01/1916	03/01/1916
War Diary	Les Brebis	04/01/1916	04/01/1916
War Diary	Loos	05/01/1916	08/01/1916
War Diary	Support Line Loos Sector	09/01/1916	12/01/1916
War Diary	Lesbrebis	13/01/1916	16/01/1916
War Diary	South Maroc	17/01/1916	24/01/1916
War Diary	Les Brebis	25/01/1916	28/01/1916
War Diary	North Maroc	29/01/1916	31/01/1916
War Diary	Sailly Labourse	01/01/1916	02/01/1916
War Diary	Houchin	03/01/1916	03/01/1916
War Diary	Les Brebis	04/01/1916	04/01/1916
War Diary	Loos	05/01/1916	08/01/1916
War Diary	Support Line Loos Sector	09/01/1916	12/01/1916
War Diary	Les Brebis	13/01/1916	16/01/1916
War Diary	South Maroc	17/01/1916	24/01/1916
War Diary	Les Brebis	25/01/1916	28/01/1916
War Diary	North Maroc	29/01/1916	31/01/1916
Miscellaneous	D.A.G 3rd Echelon	08/05/1916	08/05/1916
Heading	War Diary Of Cyclist Company 47th (London) Division Period Feby 1st-29th 8 Volume		
War Diary	North Maroc	01/02/1916	05/02/1916
War Diary	Les Brebis	06/02/1916	09/02/1916
War Diary	South Maroc	10/02/1916	11/02/1916
War Diary	Centre Sub-Section	12/02/1916	15/02/1916
War Diary	Braquemont	16/02/1916	16/02/1916
War Diary	Labuissiere	17/02/1916	17/02/1916
War Diary	Hurionville	18/02/1916	29/02/1916
Heading	War Diary Of Cyclist Company 47th (London) Division Period March 1st-31st Volume		
War Diary	Hurionville	01/03/1916	07/03/1916
War Diary	Marthes	08/03/1916	10/03/1916
War Diary	Bruay	11/03/1916	15/03/1916
War Diary	Magnicourt	16/03/1916	21/03/1916
War Diary	Hermin	22/03/1916	02/04/1916
Heading	War Diary Of The Cyclist Company 47th (London) Division For The Month Of April 1916 Vol X		
War Diary	Hermin	01/04/1916	30/04/1916
Heading	War Diary Of The Cyclist Company 47th London Division For The Month Of May 1916 Vol 10		
War Diary	Hermin	01/05/1916	09/05/1916
War Diary	Vincly	10/05/1916	10/05/1916
War Diary	Ecames	11/05/1916	29/05/1916
War Diary	Vincly	30/05/1916	30/05/1916
War Diary	Mt St Eloy	31/05/1916	31/05/1916
Heading	War Diary Of The Cyclist Company 47th (London) Division For The Month Of June 1916		
War Diary	Bois Des Alleux	01/06/1916	01/06/1916
War Diary	Mt St Eloy	02/06/1916	07/06/1916
War Diary	(Map Ref) France Sht.51c 1st Gdn 1/40000	07/06/1916	16/06/1916
War Diary	Tangry	17/06/1916	17/06/1916
War Diary	(Map Ref) Lens II 1/100000	18/06/1916	30/06/1916
Heading	War Diary Of The Cyclist Company 47th (London) Division For The Month Of July 1916 Vol 12		
War Diary	Tangry	01/07/1916	11/07/1916
War Diary	Erny St Julien	12/07/1916	12/07/1916
War Diary	Haz. 5a	13/07/1916	19/07/1916

War Diary	Erny St Julien	20/07/1916	24/07/1916
War Diary	Olhain	25/07/1916	25/07/1916
War Diary	Bois De Verdrel	26/07/1916	31/07/1916

(2) WO95/2717

March 1915 – Jul 1916

Divisional Cyclist Co

47TH DIVISION

47TH DIVL CYCLIST COMPANY

MAR 1915-JLY 1 916

47th Division

12/6357

47th Bn: Mounted troops of 47th Div
Vol I
15.3 - 31.7.15

WAR DIARY
or
INTELLIGENCE SUMMARY.
(Erase heading not required.)

Army Form C. 2118.

Instructions regarding War Diaries and Intelligence Summaries are contained in F. S. Regs., Part II and the Staff Manual respectively. Title pages will be prepared in manuscript.

Place	Date	Hour	Summary of Events and Information	Remarks and references to Appendices
	1915			
Redbourn	Mch 15	3 A.M.	Left REDBOURN for the front.	9.V.R.H
HAVRE	" 16		Arrived at HAVRE and remained overnight.	9.V.R.H
	" 17		Moved to ARQUES	9.V.R.H
ARQUES	" 18		Detained and billeted for the night	9.V.R.H
	" 19		Moved to MARLES-LES-MINES	9.V.R.H
MARLES- LES-MINES	" 20		Training	9.V.R.H
	" 21		ditto	9.V.R.H
	" 22		ditto	9.V.R.H
	" 23		ditto	9.V.R.H
	" 24		ditto	9.V.R.H
	" 25		Despatch riding started. One platoon at a time in order to arrange for communication between the H.Q's of the 4th (LONDON) BRIGADE at AUCHEL and the H.Q's of its Battalions whilst they were in the trenches. Remainder of Company Training	9.V.R.H
	" 26		ditto	9.V.R.H
	" 27		ditto	9.V.R.H
	" 28		ditto	9.V.R.H

Army Form C. 2118.

WAR DIARY
or
INTELLIGENCE SUMMARY.
(Erase heading not required.)

Instructions regarding War Diaries and Intelligence Summaries are contained in F. S. Regs., Part II. and the Staff Manual respectively. Title pages will be prepared in manuscript.

Place	Date	Hour	Summary of Events and Information	Remarks and references to Appendices
MARLES LES MINES	April 1		One platoon despatch riding, remainder training. All officers of the Company go to the Bomb Factory, BETHUNE, where they were instructed by the O.C. Bomb Factory in the making and throwing of bombs.	9.V.R. II
	" 2		One platoon despatch riding, remainder training.	9.V.R. II
	" 3		ditto	9.V.R. II
	" 4		ditto	9.V.R. II
	" 5		ditto	9.V.R. II
	" 6		ditto	9.V.R. II
	" 7		ditto	9.V.R. II
	" 8		ditto	9.V.R. II
	" 9		ditto	9.V.R. II
	" 10		ditto	9.V.R. II
	" 11		ditto	9.V.R. II
	" 12		ditto	9.V.R. II
	" 13		ditto	9.V.R. II
	" 14		ditto	9.V.R. II

WAR DIARY
or
INTELLIGENCE SUMMARY

Army Form C. 2118.

(Erase heading not required.)

Place	Date	Hour	Summary of Events and Information	Remarks and references to Appendices
MARLES-LES-MINES	April 15		One platoon despatch riding, remainder training	9.V.R. H
"	" 16		Inspected by G.O.C. 47th (LONDON) Division.	9.V.R. H
"	" 17		Battalion transport Moved to HURIONVILLE. One platoon still despatch-riding.	9.V.R. H
HURIONVILLE	" 18		Despatch-riding and training as usual	9.V.R. H
"	" 19		ditto	9.V.R. H
"	" 20		ditto	9.V.R. H
"	" 21		ditto	9.V.R. H
"	" 22		ditto	9.V.R. H
"	" 23		ditto	9.V.R. H
"	" 24		Moved to BETHUNE. Despatch-riding discontinued, but one platoon always on Divisional Guard	9.V.R. H
BETHUNE	" 25		Company permanently under two hours notice. Training continued	9.V.R. H
"	" 26		ditto	9.V.R. H
"	" 27		2 platoons spend 48 hours in the trenches (One being attached to the 6th 1st (LONDON) BRIGADE the other to the 5th (LONDON) BRIGADE) for purposes of instruction. Remainder training, except 1 one platoon on Divisional Guard.	9.V.R. H
"	" 28		2 platoons in the trenches, remainder training, except one platoon on Divisional Guard	9.V.R. H

WAR DIARY
INTELLIGENCE SUMMARY
(Erase heading not required.)

Army Form C. 2118.

Place	Date	Hour	Summary of Events and Information	Remarks and references to Appendices
BETHUNE	April 29		2 Platoons in the trenches, remainder training; except one platoon on Divisional guard.	J.V.N.L.
	30		ditto	

Army Form C. 2118.

WAR DIARY
or
INTELLIGENCE SUMMARY.
(Erase heading not required.)

Instructions regarding War Diaries and Intelligence Summaries are contained in F. S. Regs., Part II. and the Staff Manual respectively. Title pages will be prepared in manuscript.

Place	Date	Hour	Summary of Events and Information	Remarks and references to Appendices
BETHUNE	May 1st		2 Platoons in the trenches, remainder training, except one platoon on Divisional Guard.	9.V.R.1st
"	" 2nd		ditto	9.V.R.1st
"	" 3rd		ditto	9.V.R.1st
"	" 4th		ditto	9.V.R.1st
"	" 5th		ditto	9.V.R.1st
"	" 6th		ditto.	9.V.R.1st
"	" 7th		Company (less one platoon on Divisional Guard, and one platoon in the trenches) attached to the Signal Office for communication duties) move for BEUVRY	9.V.R.1st
BEUVRY	" 8th		Company (less two platoons) in constant readiness.	9.V.R.1st
"	" 9th		Moved to wood between BEUVRY and LE QUESNOY, the Company (less two platoons as above mentioned) acting with King Edwards Horse, as part of the Divisional Reserve, in a platoon of reserve bombers, in the attack made by the 1st Army Corps at FESTUBERT. 2nd Lt. Eric J. Fox invalided home.	9.V.R.1st
Wood between BEUVRY and LE QUESNOY	" 10th		Company in constant readiness.	9.V.R.1st

1577 Wt.W10791/1773 500,000 1/15 D. D. & L. A.D.S.S./Forms/C. 2118.

Army Form C. 2118.

WAR DIARY
or
INTELLIGENCE SUMMARY.

(Erase heading not required.)

Instructions regarding War Diaries and Intelligence Summaries are contained in F. S. Regs., Part II. and the Staff Manual respectively. Title pages will be prepared in manuscript.

Place	Date	Hour	Summary of Events and Information	Remarks and references to Appendices
WOOD BETWEEN BEUVRY and LE QUESNOY	May 11th		Company in contentedness	J.v.R. II
"	May 12		ditto	J.v.R. II
"	" 13		ditto	J.v.R. II
"	" 14		ditto	J.v.R. II
"	" 15		ditto	J.v.R. II
"	" 16		ditto	J.v.R. II
"	" 17		ditto	J.v.R. II
"	" 18		ditto	J.v.R. II
"	" 19		ditto	J.v.R. II
"	" 20		ditto	J.v.R. II
"	" 21		ditto	J.v.R. II
"	" 22		ditto	J.v.R. II
"	" 23		ditto	J.v.R. II
"	" 24		ditto	J.v.R. II

1577 Wt.W10791/1773 500,000 1/15 D. D. & L. A.D.S.S./Forms/C. 2118.

Army Form C. 2118.

WAR DIARY
or
INTELLIGENCE SUMMARY.
(Erase heading not required.)

Instructions regarding War Diaries and Intelligence
Summaries are contained in F.S. Regs., Part II.
and the Staff Manual respectively. Title pages
will be prepared in manuscript.

Place	Date	Hour	Summary of Events and Information	Remarks and references to Appendices
WOOD between BEUVRY and LE QUESNOY	May 25		Company (less two platoons) acted with King Edward's Horse as part of the Divisional Reserve in the attack made by the Division at GIVENCHY.	9 V.R. 25
		3-30 PM	One officer and 22 men selected from the bomb platoon left for Advanced Divisional H.Q'S. to act as the Divisional Reserve of Bombers.	
	May 26	2 P.M	The party proceeded to the trenches, being attached to the 2/7th Battalion London Regiment, and during the night of the 25th-26th were engaged in bombing operations between Lots 14 and '3. The officer in charge (Lt. H.E. GUNN) and 11 other ranks were wounded, and one other rank was killed.	
	"		Early in the morning 2nd Lt. W.J. Borkwilley was despatched to assist. Six only were used and 2nd Lt W.J. Borkwilley was slightly wounded.	
			During the night 25th-26th one officer and one platoon were on patrol work collecting stragglers.	
	" 27		State of constant readiness changed to two hours notice.	9 V.R. 25
	" 28		Nothing to report.	9 V.R. 25
	" 29		Divisional Bombing School under the supervision of the O.C. Company started.	9 V.R. 29
	" 30		Nothing to report.	9 V.R. 30

Army Form C. 2118.

WAR DIARY
or
INTELLIGENCE SUMMARY.
(Erase heading not required.)

Instructions regarding War Diaries and Intelligence Summaries are contained in F. S. Regs., Part II. and the Staff Manual respectively. Title pages will be prepared in manuscript.

Place	Date	Hour	Summary of Events and Information	Remarks. and references to Appendices
WOOD between BEUVRY and LE QUESNOY	May 31		One officer joins the Company for duty to replace casualties.	G.V.K.E

1577 Wt.W10791/1773 500,000 1/15 D. D. & L. A.D.S.S./Forms/C. 2118.

Army Form C. 2118.

WAR DIARY
or
INTELLIGENCE SUMMARY.
(Erase heading not required.)

Instructions regarding War Diaries and Intelligence Summaries are contained in F.S. Regs., Part II. and the Staff Manual respectively. Title pages will be prepared in manuscript.

Place	Date	Hour	Summary of Events and Information	Remarks and references to Appendices
Woodstown	June 1		March to VAUDRICOURT, and bivouacked in the park.	9 V.R.D.
BEUVRY and LE QUESNOY	" 2		Nothing to report	9 V.R.D.
VAUDRICOURT	" 3		4 N.C.O and 5 men attached, as permanent orderlies to Divisional Head Quarters. Divisional Guard done by platoon attached to Signal Company	9 V.R.D.
"	" 4		Nothing to report	9 V.R.D.
"	" 5		ditto	9 V.R.D.
"	" 6		2 officers of the Company were engaged, under instructions from Divisional H.Q., in reconnoitring 47th Divisional Area, and correcting map.	9 V.R.D.
"	" 7		Nothing to report.	9 V.R.D.
"	" 8		Move to NOEUX-LES-MINES	9 V.R.D.
NOEUX-LES-MINES	" 9		Nothing to report	9 V.R.D.
"	" 10		The Company took over 8 control posts under instructions from the A.P.M. One N.C.O. and 4 men were allotted to each post.	9 V.R.D.

Army Form C. 2118.

WAR DIARY
or
INTELLIGENCE SUMMARY.
(Erase heading not required.)

Instructions regarding War Diaries and Intelligence Summaries are contained in F. S. Regs., Part II. and the Staff Manual respectively. Title pages will be prepared in manuscript.

Place	Date	Hour	Summary of Events and Information	Remarks and references to Appendices
NOEUX-LES-MINES	June 11		Nothing to report.	J.V.K. Lt
"	12		ditto	J.V.K. Lt
"	13		The Officers of the Company reconnoitred the third line trenches. A cont. of 1 sect, consisting of 1 N.C.O. and 4 men, was established at DROUVIN.	J.V.K. Lt
"	14		2 officers of the Company reconnoitred the advanced second-line trenches.	J.V.K. Lt
"	15		LT. A.M. LESTER accidentally shot himself through the foot, while searching for a stray. Reconnaissance of advanced Second Line trenches finished. Divisional Bombing School under O.C. COMPANY reconstituted.	J.V.K. Lt
"	16		CAPTAIN LEMAN, and SERGEANT PARKER were wounded, 2 men of the 6th Battalion and a Sea-ef/r of the 7th Battalion were killed, through the premature explosion of a Bailey Bomb.	J.V.K. Lt
"	17	11 p.m.	2 hours notice changed to constant readiness.	
"	18		Constant readiness changed to 1 hours notice. The Bomb School course recommenced	J.V.K. Lt
			Major H. O.C. Divisional Mounted Troops took over command of Divisional Bombing School.	J.V.K. Lt

1577 Wt. W10791/1773 500,000 1/15 D.D. & L. A.D.S.S./Forms/C. 2118.

Army Form C. 2118.

WAR DIARY
or
INTELLIGENCE SUMMARY.
(Erase heading not required.)

Instructions regarding War Diaries and Intelligence Summaries are contained in F. S. Regs., Part II. and the Staff Manual respectively. Title pages will be prepared in manuscript.

Place	Date	Hour	Summary of Events and Information	Remarks and references to Appendices
NOEEUX LES MINES	January 19		Nothing to report	J.V.K. 25
"	" 20		ditto	J.V.K. 25
"	" 21		ditto	J.V.K. 25
"	" 22		State of 1 hours notice changed to that of 2 hours.	J.V.K. 25
"	" 23		1st reinforcement consisting of 2 N.C.O'S and 10 men joined for duty to replace casualties	J.V.K. 25
"	" 24		Nothing to report	J.V.K. 25
"	" 25		ditto	
"	" 26		ditto	
"	" 27		6 Head Quarters orderlies and B Platoon (attached to Signal Company) returned to totally Company for duty. Sgt. NAPIER awarded D.C.M. for conspicuous bravery during the operations of the 25TH - 26TH of May	J.V.K. 15
"	" 28		Nothing to report	J.V.K. 25
"	" 29		N.V.K. Control posts reduced to 1 N.C.O and 3 men per post	J.V.K. 25
"	" 30		LT MURPHY and 3 officers attending for instructions were wounded during course at BOMB SCHOOL	J.V.K. 35

1577 Wt.W10791/1773 500,000 1/15 D. D. & L. A.D.S.S./Forms/C. 2118.

Army Form C. 2118.

WAR DIARY
or
INTELLIGENCE SUMMARY.
(Erase heading not required.)

Instructions regarding War Diaries and Intelligence Summaries are contained in F. S. Regs., Part II. and the Staff Manual respectively. Title pages will be prepared in manuscript.

Place	Date	Hour	Summary of Events and Information	Remarks and references to Appendices
NOEUX-LES-MINES	July 1		Nothing to report	J.V.R.25
"	" 2		ditto	J.V.R.25
"	" 3		ditto	J.V.R.25
"	" 4		ditto	J.V.R.25
"	" 5		ditto	J.V.R.25
"	" 6		ditto	J.V.R.25
"	" 7		ditto	J.V.R.25
"	" 8		ditto	J.V.R.25
"	" 9		A. Platoon went to trenches (Sector X) for 72 hours	J.V.R.25
"	" 10		Nothing to report	J.V.R.25
"	" 11		ditto	J.V.R.25
"	" 12		Company moved to HESDIGNEUL, bivouacking close to King Edwards Horse.	J.V.R.25
HESDIGNEUL	" 13		Nothing to report	J.V.R.25
"	" 14		Company returned to NOEUX-LES-MINES	J.V.R.25
NOEUX-LES-MINES	" 15		F Platoon (Bomb Platoon) go to the trenches for 72 hours	J.V.R.25

Army Form C. 2118.

WAR DIARY
or
INTELLIGENCE SUMMARY.
(Erase heading not required.)

Instructions regarding War Diaries and Intelligence Summaries are contained in F. S. Regs., Part II. and the Staff Manual respectively. Title pages will be prepared in manuscript.

Place	Date	Hour	Summary of Events and Information	Remarks and references to Appendices
NOEUX-LES-MINES	July 16		Nothing to report	9th V.K. 25
"	" 17		ditto	9 V.K. 25
"	" 18		2 Platoon go to the trenches for 72 hours	9 V.K. 25
"	" 19		O.C. Company made a reconnaissance of the French lines at CALONNE	9 V.K. 25
"	" 20		B Platoon go to the trenches for 72 hours	9 V.K. 25
"	" 21		Nothing to report	9 V.K. 25
"	" 22		An officer of the bicyclist Company makes a reconnaissance of the French Lines at CALONNE	9 V.K. 25
"	" 23		Nothing to report.	9 V.K. 25
"	" 24		D Platoon go to the trenches for 72 hours	9 V.K. 25
"	" 25		Nothing to report	9 V.K. 25
"	" 26		ditto	9 V.K. 25
"	" 27		ditto	9 V.K. 25
"	" 28		ditto	9 V.K. 25
"	" 29		2 officers of the Company made a reconnaissance of the French trenches at CALONNE	9 V.K. 25

1577 Wt.W10791/1773 500,000 1/15 D. D. & L.   A.D.S.S./Forms/C. 2118.

Army Form C. 2118.

WAR DIARY
or
INTELLIGENCE SUMMARY.
(Erase heading not required.)

Instructions regarding War Diaries and Intelligence Summaries are contained in F.S. Regs., Part II. and the Staff Manual respectively. Title pages will be prepared in manuscript.

Place	Date	Hour	Summary of Events and Information	Remarks and references to Appendices
NOEUX-LES-MINES	July 30		Nothing to report	g.v.r.21
"	" 31		ditto	g.v.r.21

121/6550

47th Division

47th Cyclist Coy.
Vol II
From 1st to 31st August 1915

Army Form C. 2118.

WAR DIARY
or
INTELLIGENCE SUMMARY.
(Erase heading not required.)

Instructions regarding War Diaries and Intelligence Summaries are contained in F. S. Regs., Part II. and the Staff Manual respectively. Title pages will be prepared in manuscript.

Place	Date	Hour	Summary of Events and Information	Remarks and references to Appendices
NOEUX-LES-MINES	Aug. 1		9 control posts taken over by the 15th Divisional Cyclist Company. Control Post established at MARLES-LES-MINES, consisting of 1 officer, 3 N.C.O's, and 15 men.	9 V. K. II
"	Aug. 2		Company move to N.E. corner of the BOIS DES DAMES, where they bivouack. A Captain joins the Company for duty to replace casualties. The Company is now in Corps Reserve.	9 V. K. II / 9 V. R. II
BOIS DES DAMES	Aug. 3		Three officers (3 Lieutenants) join the company for duty to replace casualties.	9 V. K. II
"	Aug. 4		Nothing to report.	9 V. K. II
"	Aug. 5		ditto	9 V. K. II
"	6		Training (Drill)	9 V. R. II
"	7		Nothing to report	9 V. R. II
"	8		Control posts at MARLES-LES-MINES taken over by King Edward's Horse. A control Post consisting of 1 N.C.O and 4 men, established at FONTENELLE FARM.	9 V. K. II / 9 V. R. II
"	9		Nothing to report	9 W. R. II
"	10		ditto	9 V. R. II
"	11		Training (Drill)	9 V. K. II
"	12		Training (an attack scheme consisting of three columns, fighting a delaying action against a skeleton enemy)	9 V. K. II
"	13		Training (clearing villages)	9 V. K. II

Army Form C. 2118.

WAR DIARY
or
INTELLIGENCE SUMMARY.
(Erase heading not required.)

Place	Date	Hour	Summary of Events and Information	Remarks and references to Appendices
BOIS DES DAMES	Aug 14		FONTENELLE FARM post relieved (taken over by KING EDWARDS HORSE), and company relieve KING EDWARDS HORSE at MARLES-LES-MINES – post role is reversed.	J.U.K.H.
"	" 15		This exchange of posts is to take place weekly until further notice.	J.U.K.H.
"	" 16		Training	J.U.K.H.
"	" 17		ditto (BOMB PLATOON and SCOUTS undergo special training. Remainder of the company go route-march) J.U.K.H.	J.U.K.H.
"	" 18		ditto (ditto)	J.U.K.H.
"	" 19		ditto	J.U.K.H.
"	" 20		ditto	J.U.K.H.
"	" 21		Training (Drill and Interior Economy)	J.U.K.H.
"	" 22		Nothing to Report.	J.U.K.H.
"	" 23		Training (4th of the Company acted as enemy while the remainder of the had to locate and attack them)	J.U.K.H.
"	" 24		Training (Advance guard work and inter-communication between parallel roads)	J.U.K.H.
"	" 25		ditto (inter-communication between parallel roads)	J.U.K.H.
"	" 26		ditto (Rear-guard work)	J.U.K.H.

Army Form C. 2118.

WAR DIARY
or
INTELLIGENCE SUMMARY.
(Erase heading not required.)

CYCLIST COMPANY,
DIVISIONAL MOUNTED TROOPS,
47th (LONDON) DIVISION.

Place	Date	Hour	Summary of Events and Information	Remarks and references to Appendices
BOIS DES DAMES	Aug 27		Training (reconnaissance work). The Company take over 5 Straggler's Posts and 1 Control Post (1 N.C.O. and 4 men per post, the posts being relieved every week)	J.V.K.II
"	" 28		Company dig trenches for Divisional Bombing School.	J.V.K.II
"	" 29		ditto	J.V.K.II
"	" 30		ditto. Company move to NOEUX-LES-MINES.	J.V.K.II
NOEUX-LES-MINES	" 31		ditto	J.V.K.II
"			ditto	J.V.K.II

121/7083

47th Division

47th Div: Cyclist Cy
Vol III
Sept. 15

Army Form C. 2118.

WAR DIARY
or
INTELLIGENCE SUMMARY.
(Erase heading not required.)

Instructions regarding War Diaries and Intelligence Summaries are contained in F. S. Regs., Part II. and the Staff Manual respectively. Title pages will be prepared in manuscript.

Place	Date	Hour	Summary of Events and Information	Remarks and references to Appendices
NOEUX-LES-MINES	Sept. 1		Company dig trenches for Divisional Bomb School.	g.v.r.d.
"	" 2		ditto	g.v.r.d.
"	" 3		ditto	g.v.r.d.
"	" 4		ditto	g.v.r.d.
"	" 5		Nothing to Report	g.v.r.d.
"	" 6		ditto	g.v.r.d.
"	" 7	12 noon	The Company take over 8 new Traffic Control Posts.	g.v.r.d.
"	" 8		Nothing to Report	g.v.r.d.
"	" 9		ditto	g.v.r.d.
"	" 10		The personell of the Control Posts is relieved by convalescents except for 29 N.C.O's and men, but the posts still remain under the supervision of the seconded in command and 2 subaltern officers. The remainder of the Company is now engaged in digging a down communication trench between W3 and the advanced second line of trenches.	g.v.r.d. and g.v.r.d.
"	" 11		Company digging.	g.v.r.d.

WAR DIARY
or
INTELLIGENCE SUMMARY.
(Erase heading not required.)

Army Form C. 2118.

Place	Date	Hour	Summary of Events and Information	Remarks and references to Appendices
NOEUX-LES-MINES	12		Company digging	9 v.K.21
"	13		ditto	9 v.K.21
"	14		ditto	9 v.K.21
"	15		ditto	9 v.K.21
"	16		ditto	9 v.K.21
"	17		ditto	9 v.K.21
"	18		ditto	9 v.K.21
"	19		ditto	9 v.K.21
"	20		ditto. Company take over six new control posts.	9 v.K.21
"	21		ditto	9 v.K.21
"	22		ditto	9 v.K.21
"	23		Company move to HOUCHIN	9 v.K.21
HOUCHIN	24		Company move to field near MAZINGARBE. One officer and 44 men are detailed for escorting German prisoners; one officer and 20 men from to v.K. at LES BREBIS, and 2 parties of 12 O.R. to serve the exits of the communication trenches in MAROC. One Battle post...	9 v.K.21

Army Form C. 2118.

WAR DIARY
or
INTELLIGENCE SUMMARY.

(Erase heading not required.)

Instructions regarding War Diaries and Intelligence Summaries are contained in F.S. Regs., Part II. and the Staff Manual respectively. Title pages will be prepared in manuscript.

Place	Date	Hour	Summary of Events and Information	Remarks and references to Appendices
FIELD NEAR MAZINGARBE	Sept 24		also established	
	" 25		2 officers and 10 men are detailed for escorting German Prisoners, in addition to the original G.V.K.IT. number.	G.V.K.IT
	" 26		Company move to LES BREBIS. A draft of 25 N.C.O's and men arrive from the base.	G.V.K.IT
LES BREBIS	" 27	19 a.m	All officers and men on duty escorting German Prisoners are recalled.	G.V.K.IT
"	" 28		Company in a state of readiness of one hour. One officer wounded whilst estimating the number of Germans.	G.V.K.IT
"	" 29		Company engaged in salvaging the English and German front lines, as held before the attack of September 25th. Company (less Head-quarters) move to NORTH MAROC	G.V.K.IT
"	" 30		ditto. Company Head-quarters move to NORTH MAROC	G.V.K.IT
		5 p.m	Company bury ten English and French dead in the W3 area.	G.V.K.IT

(signature) Capt
CYCLIST COMPANY,
47th (LONDON) DIVISION.

121/7358

47th Division

47th cyclist ...
for IV
Oct 15

Army Form C. 2118.

WAR DIARY
or
INTELLIGENCE SUMMARY.
(Erase heading not required.)

Instructions regarding War Diaries and Intelligence Summaries are contained in F. S. Regs., Part II and the Staff Manual respectively. Title pages will be prepared in manuscript.

Place	Date	Hour	Summary of Events and Information	Remarks and references to Appendices
NORTH MAROC	Oct. 1		Company bury English and French dead in W3 area.	9. V.R.2t
"	" 2		Company move to wood near GOSNAY	9. V.R.2t
WOOD NEAR	" 3		Nothing to report	9. V.R.2t
GOSNAY	" 4		Move to LABEUVRIERE	9. V.R.2t
LABEUVRIERE	" 5		Nothing to report.	9. V.R.2t
"	" 6		Move to NOEUX-LES-MINES. Company take over 4 control posts.	9. V.R.2t
NOEUX-LES-	" 7		Nothing to report.	9. V.R.2t
MINES	" 8		Nothing to report 2nd Lieut. E.B BURY attached to the 13TH Battn. London Regt. for	9. V.R.2t
"	" 9		duty. Company inspected by G.O.C. 4TH CORPS.	9. V.R.2t
"	" 10		Nothing to report	9. V.R.2t
"	" 11	3 P.M.	2 officers and 50 men move to NORTH MAROC, in order to salvage the original front line trenches of W3 of all ammunition, arms, and equipment	9. V.R.2t
"		6 P.M.	Company in a state of constant readiness.	9. V.R.2t
"	" 12		2 officers and 50 men still engaged on salvage work	9. V.R.2t

1577 Wt. W10791/1773 500,000 1/15 D. D. & L. A.D.S.S./Forms/C. 2118.

WAR DIARY
or
INTELLIGENCE SUMMARY.
(Erase heading not required.)

Army Form C. 2118.

Place	Date	Hour	Summary of Events and Information	Remarks and references to Appendices
	1915			
NOEUX-LES-MINES	Oct.13		Company take over two Battle Straggler's Posts. 2nd Lt. C.E. JAY transferred to hospital.	J.W.R.Lt
"	" 14		Battle Stragglers posts dismissed. Company take over a guardson & a front and an ammunition depot.	J.W.R.Lt
"	" 15		Company move to MAZINGARBE. K.M. Company relieved of 4 control posts, taken over on October 6th.	J.W.R.Lt
"	" 16		Nothing to report.	J.W.R.Lt
"	" 17		Captain B.T.WARD attached to 20TH BATT, LONDON REGT. for 1 month.	J.W.R.Lt
"	" 18		Company engaged in burying the dead and salvaging arms, ammunition, equipment etc. in area directly west of LOOS including the (BETHUNE – LENS road).	J.W.R.Lt
"	" 19		ditto	J.W.R.Lt
"	" 20		Company engaged on salvage work and burying dead hyites.	J.W.R.Lt
"	" 21		Company engaged in salvaging the original German front trenches.	J.W.R.Lt
"	" 22		Company engaged in salvage work.	J.W.R.Lt
"	" 23		Company engaged on salvaging German live shells.	J.W.R.Lt
"	" 24		ditto	J.W.R.Lt

Army Form C. 2118.

WAR DIARY
or
INTELLIGENCE SUMMARY.
(Erase heading not required.)

Instructions regarding War Diaries and Intelligence Summaries are contained in F. S. Regs., Part II. and the Staff Manual respectively. Title pages will be prepared in manuscript.

Place	Date	Hour	Summary of Events and Information	Remarks and references to Appendices
MAZINGARBE	Oct 25		Company engaged in night digging.	G.V.R. 25
"	" 26		1 officer and 20 men digging.	G.V.R. 25
"	" 27		ditto	G.V.R. 25
"	" 28		1 officer and 20 men digging. 1 officer and 42 men do salvage work in LOOS.	G.V.R. 25
"	" 29		ditto	G.V.R. 25
"	" 30		1 officer and 20 men digging. 1 officer and 30 men do salvage work near LOOS.	G.V.R. 25
"	" 31		1 officer and 20 men digging.	G.V.R. 25

[signature] Capt
Omdg. Cyclist Company,
Divisional Mounted Troops,
4) (London) Division.

1 NOV 1915

Appeal Co. 47th Dn.

1892

Vol V

12/7694

Army Form C. 2118.

WAR DIARY
or
INTELLIGENCE SUMMARY.
(Erase heading not required.)

Instructions regarding War Diaries and Intelligence Summaries are contained in F. S. Regs., Part II. and the Staff Manual respectively. Title pages will be prepared in manuscript.

Place	Date	Hour	Summary of Events and Information	Remarks and references to Appendices
MAZINGARBE	Mar. 2		One platoon engaged in salvaging at Loos Redoubt.	W.9.b.2.oft
"	3		One officer and 90 men trench digging at 65 metre Point. Loading party of one officer & 20 men at VICTORIA STATION. Six reinforcements arrived.	"
"	4		One officer & 20 men trench digging at 65 metre Point. Railway working party at Victoria Station & Loven Station.	"
"	5		One officer & 20 men trench digging at 65 metre Point.	"
"	6		" " " " "	"
"	7		Inspected by Major T. London. 2nd Lt. Murphy rejoined for duty. Sgt. Napier received the Medaille Militaire.	"
"	8		One officer & 20 men trench digging at 65 metre Point.	"
"	9		" " " " "	title 2nd Lt.
"	10		" " " " "	"
"	11		One officer & 20 men trench digging at 65 metre Point also 2 officers & 25 men salvaging at Loos Redoubt. Two new officers joined for duty from the 3/2nd Ln. Div. Cyclist Company.	title

Army Form C. 2118.

WAR DIARY
or
INTELLIGENCE SUMMARY.
(Erase heading not required.)

Instructions regarding War Diaries and Intelligence Summaries are contained in F. S. Regs., Part II and the Staff Manual respectively. Title pages will be prepared in manuscript.

Place	Date	Hour	Summary of Events and Information	Remarks and references to Appendices
MAZINGARBE	Nov. 12		1 officer and 20 men salvaging at LOOS REDOUBT. 1 officer and 2 platoons move to LABEUVRIERE for trench digging for Divisional Bomb School.	J.V.R.II
"	Nov. 13		Nothing to report.	J.V.R.II
"	" 14		Company move to HURIONVILLE (in Corps Reserve). 1 officer and 2 platoons return from LABEUVRIERE. One officer and 10 men go to Divisional Bomb School for one week's instruction.	J.V.R.II J.V.R.II
HURIONVILLE	Nov. 15		Nothing to report.	J.V.R.II
"	" 16		Company dig trenches for Divisional Bomb School near LABEUVRIERE.	J.V.R.II
"	" 17		ditto	J.V.R.II
"	" 18		ditto	J.V.R.II
"	" 19		ditto	J.V.R.II
"	" 20		ditto	J.V.R.II
"	" 21		Nothing to report.	J.V.R.II
"	" 22		Company dig trenches for Divisional Bomb School near LABEUVRIERE. One officer and 10 men go to Divisional Bomb School for one week's instruction.	J.V.R.II

WAR DIARY
or
INTELLIGENCE SUMMARY.

Army Form C. 2118.

Place	Date	Hour	Summary of Events and Information	Remarks and references to Appendices
HURIONVILLE	Nov 23		Company dig trenches for Divisional Bomb School near LABEUVRIERE.	9.V.R.21
"	" 24		ditto	9.V.R.21
"	" 25		ditto	9.V.R.21
"	" 26		ditto	9.V.R.21
"	" 27		Nothing to report.	9.V.R.21
"	" 28		ditto	9.V.R.21
"	" 29		ditto	9.V.R.21
"	" 30		ditto	9.V.R.21
"	Dec 1		Company take part in a Divisional Exercise and billet for the night at	
"	" 2	5.30 A.M.	Company leave , and take part in the Divisional Exercise until 9 A.M. At which operations ceased and the Company returned to HURIONVILLE	

CYGNET COMPANY.
47 (LONDON) DIVISION

47th Cyclist Co.

Dec / Vol VI

Army Form C. 2118.

WAR DIARY
or
INTELLIGENCE SUMMARY.
(Erase heading not required.)

Place	Date	Hour	Summary of Events and Information	Remarks and references to Appendices
HURIONVILLE	Dec 1		Company take part in a Divisional Exercise, and billet for the night at LIGNE	g.v.R.21
LIGNE	" 2	5-30 A.M.	Company leave LIGNE. Operations continued till 9 A.M., when company return to HURIONVILLE.	g.v.R.21
HURIONVILLE	" 3		Company move to NOEUX-LES-MINES and are attached to the 1ST DIVISION for administration.	g.v.R.21
NOEUX-LES-MINES	" 4		Company are engaged in repairing the SAILLY-LABOURSE and GRENAY lines under the supervision of the 25TH A.T. Company R.E. and the 132TH A.T. Company R.E. respectively.	g.v.R.21
"	" 5		ditto. One officer and 10 men go to Divisional Bomb School for weekinstruction.	g.v.R.21
"	" 6		ditto	g.v.R.21
"	" 7		ditto	g.v.R.21
"	" 8		ditto	g.v.R.21
"	" 9		ditto	g.v.R.21
"	" 10		ditto	g.v.R.21
"	" 11		ditto	g.v.R.21

WAR DIARY
or
INTELLIGENCE SUMMARY.

(Erase heading not required.)

Army Form C. 2118.

Place	Date	Hour	Summary of Events and Information	Remarks and references to Appendices
NOEUX-LES-MINES	Dec 12		Company engaged in repairing the SAILLY LABOURSE and GRENAY lines.	9.U.R.Lt.
			1 Captain attached to 20th Battalion London Regt from this unit returns to duty	9.U.R.Lt
	13		ditto	9.U.R.Lt
	14		Nothing to report.	9.U.R.Lt.
	15		Company move to DROUVIN.	9.U.R.Lt.
	16		Nothing to report	9.U.R.Lt
	17		ditto	9.U.R.Lt
	18		ditto	9.U.R.Lt
	19		Company move to LABOURSE and are attached (less 2 platoons and all cycles) to the 19th Batt. London Regt (141st Bde.) for tactical purposes	9.U.R.Lt
	20		Nothing to report.	9.U.R.Lt.
	21		ditto	9.U.R.Lt
	22		ditto	9.U.R.Lt
	23		Company move to SAILLY-LABOURSE and are Brigade Reserve. One platoon is attached	9.U.R.Lt
	24		9.U.K. Attached to the R.E for duty. The second in command is attached to the 18th LON.REGT. for service in the trenches as second-in-command and to take charge of the firing line. The front platoons march up the line as Brigade Bombers. They arrange their own relief, every 48 hours.	9.U.R.Lt 9.U.R.Lt

WAR DIARY or INTELLIGENCE SUMMARY.

Army Form C. 2118.

(Erase heading not required.)

Place	Date	Hour	Summary of Events and Information	Remarks and references to Appendices
SAILLY-LABOURSE	Dec.24	3-20A.M	(less grenadier platoon and 2 platoons at DROUVIN) Company move to LANCASHIRE TRENCH with the 19TH LON.REGT. and take up their position on the left of their line (Position is G.2.B.3-10 (map ref. 1/10,000 36c N.W.3) The company are in a state of constant readiness, in case of an enemy attack, which was expected after the blowing up of a mine in the HOGS BACK at 7-12 A.M.	J.V.R.2L
LANCASHIRE TRENCH	Dec 25	4.45 p.m.	Company move to CLARKS KEEP (VERMELLES) to draw Gum Boots and from there to NORTHAMPTON TRENCH (Position is approximately G.4.B.3-0 (map ref 1/10,000 36c N.W.3) and relieve right platoon of C.CO. 18TH LON.REGT and left platoon of D CO.18TH LON. REGT. Relief was not completed till 1 A.M, owing to the muddy state of the trenches.	J.V.R.2L
NORTHAMPTON TRENCH	Dec.26		Nothing to Report	J.V.R.2L
"	" 27		ditto	J.V.R.2L
"	" 28	10 A.M.	Company move to LANCASHIRE TRENCH and	J.V.R.2L
LANCASHIRE	" 29		Nothing to report.	J.V.R.2L
LANCASHIRE TRENCH	" 30	7-15A.M	1/2 Company (less platoons shown above) to NORTHAMPTON TRENCH as before, and 1/2 Company take up position in SACKVILLE STREET as Reserve Company of the 20TH LON.REGT, who are on the immediate right of the 19TH LON.REGT.	J.V.R.2L
		7-15 P.M.	An enemy mine is blown up in the adjoining sector on our right, held by the 143rd Bde. This was followed by an intense bombardment lasting 30 minutes	J.V.R.2L

Army Form C. 2118.

WAR DIARY
or
INTELLIGENCE SUMMARY.
(Erase heading not required.)

Place	Date	Hour	Summary of Events and Information	Remarks and references to Appendices
D.2 SECTOR	Dec. 31		Company move to SAILLY-LABOURSE and are in DIV. Reserve.	J.v.R.II

Cyclist Coy 47 Div
Jan
Vol. II/5

- 47

Cyclist Coy.
Vol VI

Army Form C. 2118.

WAR DIARY
or
INTELLIGENCE SUMMARY.
(Erase heading not required.)

Instructions regarding War Diaries and Intelligence Summaries are contained in F. S. Regs., Part II. and the Staff Manual respectively. Title pages will be prepared in manuscript.

Place	Date	Hour	Summary of Events and Information	Remarks and references to Appendices
SAILLY-LABOURSE	Jan.1		Nothing to report.	G.V.R. Lt
"	Jan.2		Company move to HOUCHIN. The 2 platoons at DROUVIN replace 2 of the platoons who have been in the trenches.	G.V.R. Lt
HOUCHIN	Jan.3	11 A.M.	Company move to LES BREBIS. On arrival in billeting area B company sustain through the explosion of an enemy shell.	G.V.R. Lt
		5.30 A.M.	2 officers go to LES BREBIS to make a reconnaissance of the line to be taken over by the company.	G.V.R. Lt
LES BREBIS	Jan.4	6.45 P.M.	The two platoons attached to the 20TH Bn. LONDON REGT, move off in rear of that Battalion.	G.V.R. Lt
		7.30 P.M.	The remaining two platoons and H.Q.'s move to billets in LOOS	G.V.R. Lt
LOOS	Jan.5		Nothing to report.	G.V.R. Lt
"	Jan.6		One platoon under the second-in-command moves into the line as support platoon to the centre company of the 19TH London Regiment (position is G.36.b.6.2 to G.36.b.D.2-8. ref 1/10,000 map Sheet B (pt) No 28). Unit on left of 19TH LONDON REGIMENT is SOUTH WALES BORDERERS (1ST DIV.), and unit on right is 18TH LONDON REGIMENT. Grenadier platoon remains with O.C. COMPANY at LOOS. LOOS SECTOR	G.V.R. Lt G.V.R. Lt

Army Form C. 2118.

WAR DIARY
or
INTELLIGENCE SUMMARY.

(Erase heading not required.)

Instructions regarding War Diaries and Intelligence
Summaries are contained in F. S. Regs., Part II.
and the Staff Manual respectively. Title pages
will be prepared in manuscript.

Place	Date	Hour	Summary of Events and Information	Remarks and references to Appendices
LOOS	Jan.7		Nothing to report.	g.v.R.25
"	Jan.8	6.p.m.	Platoon attached to 19th Bn. London Regiment returns to LOOS	g.v.R.25
		10.p.m	This platoon and ½ grenadier platoon take up left of support position between LOOS — FOSSE 12 road and BETHUNE-LENS road. The 2 platoons attached to 20th since Jan.4th and ½ grenadier platoon, hold right of support position (position is from M.6.a.0.4 to M.6.8.A.6-7 ref 1/19,088 map Secret Body No 28). Company act as support to left company of 20th. The unit on left of 20th is the 17th LONDON REGT. The unit on the right is the 142nd Bde.	g.v.R.25 g.v.R.25 g.v.R.25 g.v.R.25 g.v.R.25 g.v.R.25
SUPPORT LINE, LOOS SECTOR	Jan.9		Nothing to report.	g.v.R.25
"	Jan.10		13th Bn. LONDON REGT relieve 20th Bn. LONDON REGT.	g.v.R.25
"	Jan.11		Nothing to report.	g.v.R.25
"	Jan.12	8.p.m.	Company move to LES BREBIS and are in Divisional Reserve.	g.v.R.25
LES BREBIS	Jan.13		Nothing to report.	g.v.R.25
"	Jan.14		ditto	g.v.R.25
"	" 15		ditto	g.v.R.25

Army Form C. 2118.

WAR DIARY
or
INTELLIGENCE SUMMARY.
(Erase heading not required.)

Instructions regarding War Diaries and Intelligence Summaries are contained in F.S. Regs., Part II. and the Staff Manual respectively. Title pages will be prepared in manuscript.

Place	Date	Hour	Summary of Events and Information	Remarks and references to Appendices
LES BREBIS	Jan. 16TH	4.30 P.M.	Company move into MAROC centre sub-section. 2 platoons are attached to the 18TH Batt. LON. REGT and are in the front line (garrison 1 platoon on the North West half of the NORTHERN CRASSIER;	J.V.R.LT
			1 platoon on the extreme western end of the SOUTHERN CRASSIER) 2 platoons and H.Qs remain in support at S. MAROC.	J.V.R.LT
SOUTH MAROC	" 17TH		17TH BATT. LON. REGT open on right flank RB, 19TH BATT. LON. REGT also on left. Nothing to report.	J.V.R.LT
"	" 18TH		20TH Batt. LON. REGT relieve 18TH Batt. LON. REGT; otherwise the situation remains unchanged.	J.V.R.LT
"	" 19TH		State Nothing to report	J.V.R.LT
"	" 20TH		2 platoons in support relieve 2 platoons in front line (now with 20TH Bn. LON. REGT.) 19TH Batt. LON. REGT are on the left flank, 17TH Batt. LON. REGT on the right flank.	J.V.R.LT
"	" 21ST		Nothing to report.	J.V.R.LT
"	" 22ND		19TH Batt. LON. REGT are relieved by 18TH Batt. LON. REGT.; otherwise the situation remains unchanged.	J.V.R.LT
"	" 23RD		Nothing to report.	J.V.R.LT
"	" 24TH	6 P.M.	Company move into Divisional Reserve at LES BREBIS	J.V.R.LT
LES BREBIS	" 25TH		Nothing to report.	J.V.R.LT
"	" 26TH		ditto	J.V.R.LT
"	" 27TH		ditto	J.V.R.LT

WAR DIARY
or
INTELLIGENCE SUMMARY.

Army Form C. 2118.

Place	Date	Hour	Summary of Events and Information	Remarks and references to Appendices
LES BREBIS	Jan. 28	5.30 p.m.	One platoon moves into the LOOS SECTOR J.V.H. and is attached to C Coy. 19TH Bn. LONDON REGT. (position approximately from M6a 1.2 to M6a2B Ref. 1 map, Secret copy No 23). 20TH Bn. LON. REGT. on right flank, 18TH Bn. LON. REGT. on left. Three platoons and H.Q's move into support at NORTH MAROC and are attached to 19TH Bn. LON. REGT.	J.V.H. Lt. J.V.H. Lt
NORTH MAROC	Jan. 29	night	Nothing to report.	J.V.H. Lt
"	" 30	night	One platoon event transport from LES BREBIS to LOOS etc. They then dig for 2 hours, and carry up rations to the front line trenches, - under the instructions of the 19TH Bn. LON. REGT. 2 platoons widen and deepen PICCADILLY TRENCH under the instructions of the 2/3rd Field Co. R.E.	J.V.H. Lt
"	" 31	night	3 platoons are engaged in repairing a communication trench in the 19TH Bn's sub-section	J.V.H. Lt J.V. R.H.

1577 Wt.W10791/1773 500,000 1/15 D. D. & L. A.D.S.S./Forms/C. 2118.

WAR DIARY
or
INTELLIGENCE SUMMARY.
(Erase heading not required.)

Army Form C. 2118.

Instructions regarding War Diaries and Intelligence Summaries are contained in F.S. Regs., Part II. and the Staff Manual respectively. Title pages will be prepared in manuscript.

Copy

Place	Date	Hour	Summary of Events and Information	Remarks and references to Appendices
SAILLY LABOURSE	Jan 1.		Nothing to report.	All entries made by J.V. Knox Lt.
"	Jan 2		Company moves to HOUCHIN. The two platoons at DROUVIN replace 20th platoons who have been in the trenches.	
HOUCHIN.	Jan 3.	11 AM	Company moves to LES BREBIS. On arrival in billeting area Company sustain one casualties through the explosion of an enemy shell.	
LES BREBIS	Jan 4.	5.30 AM	2 Officers go to LES BREBIS to make a reconnaissance of the line to be taken over by the Company.	
		6.45 pm	The two platoons attached to the 20th Bn LONDON REGT move off in rear of that battalion.	
		7.30 pm	The remaining two platoons and HQ move to billets in LOOS	
LOOS	Jan 5		Nothing to report.	
"	Jan 6.		One Platoon under the Reconn. Comma'd moves into LOOS SECTOR in support platoon to the Centre Company of the 19th London Regiment (Garrison is G.34.D.6-6 to G.36.D.8-8.M) to two maps Secret Copy (No 28). Sent on left of 19th LONDON REGIMENT to SOUTH WALES BORDERERS (1st Div) and moved on right to 18th LONDON REGIMENT Grenadier platoon remains with O.C. COMPANY at LOOS.	
"	Jan 7.		Nothing to report.	
"	Jan 8	6/30 am	Platoon attached to 19th Bn London Regt. Returns to LOOS	

Army Form C. 2118.

WAR DIARY
or
INTELLIGENCE SUMMARY.
(Erase heading not required.)

Copy

Instructions regarding War Diaries and Intelligence Summaries are contained in F. S. Regs., Part II. and the Staff Manual respectively. Title pages will be prepared in manuscript.

Place	Date	Hour	Summary of Events and Information	Remarks and references to Appendices
LOOS	Jan 8	10 p.m.	The platoon and 2 Grenadier platoon take up left of support position between LOOS-FOSSE 12 road and BETHUNE-LENS road. The 2 platoons attached to the 20th since Jan 1st and 2 Grenadier platoon, hold right of support position (position to from M6 A0-4 to M6 A6-7 inf 15.000 map sheet 36c No 28) Company act in support to left company of 20th, 2 the unit on left of 20th is the 17th LONDON REGIMENT. The unit on the right is the 142nd BDE.	All entries made by J.V. Knox Lt
SUPPORT LINE. LOOS SECTOR	Jan 9		Nothing to report. 18th Bn LONDON REGT. relieve 20th Bn LONDON REGT.	
"	Jan 10		Nothing to report.	
"	Jan 11	8 p.m.	Company move to LES BREBIS and are in Divisional Reserve.	
LES BREBIS	Jan 13		Nothing to report.	
"	14		Ditto	
"	15		Ditto.	
"	16	4.30 p.m.	Company move into MAROC Centre sub section. 2 platoons are attached to the 18th Batt LON. REGT., and are in the front line (position 1 platoon on the left half of the NORTHERN CRASSIER. 1 platoon on the extreme western end of the SOUTHERN CRASSIER.) 2 platoons and HQs remain in support in S. MAROC. 17th Batt LON. REGT. are on right flank; 19th Batt. LON. REGT. are on left.	

Army Form C. 2118.

WAR DIARY
or
INTELLIGENCE SUMMARY.

(Erase heading not required.)

Instructions regarding War Diaries and Intelligence Summaries are contained in F.S. Regs., Part II. and the Staff Manual respectively. Title pages will be prepared in manuscript.

Copy.

Place	Date	Hour	Summary of Events and Information	Remarks and references to Appendices
SOUTH MAROC	Jan 17th		Nothing to report.	All entries made by J.J. Knox Lt.
"	18th		20th Batt. LON REGT. relieve 18th Batt. LON REGT. otherwise the situation remains unchanged.	
"	19th		Nothing to report.	
"	20th		2 platoons in support relieve 2 platoons in front line (now with 20th Bn. LON. REGT:) 19th Bn. LON: REGT: are on the left flank, 17th Bn. LON. REGT. on the right flank.	
"	21st		Nothing to report.	
"	22nd		19th Bn. LON REGT. are relieved by 18th Bn. LON. REGT: otherwise the situation remains unchanged.	
"	23rd		Nothing to report.	
"	24th	6.pm	Company move into Divisional Reserve at LES BREBIS.	
LES BREBIS	25th		Nothing to report	
"	26th		ditto.	
"	27th		ditto.	
"	28th		One platoon move into the front line trenches of the LOOS SECTOR and is attached to C Coy. 19th Bn. LON. REGT (position approximately from M.6.a.1.2. to M.6.a.2.3. Puits map 10:10,000 New Copy No 25). 20th Bn. LON. REGT. on right flank, 18th Bn. LON. REGT. on left. Three platoons and H.Q. move into support at NORTH MAROC and are attached to 19th Bn LON. REGT.	

Army Form C. 2118.

WAR DIARY
or
INTELLIGENCE SUMMARY.

(Erase heading not required.)

Instructions regarding War Diaries and Intelligence Summaries are contained in F.S. Regs., Part II. and the Staff Manual respectively. Title pages will be prepared in manuscript.

copy

Place	Date	Hour	Summary of Events and Information	Remarks and references to Appendices
NORTH MAROC	Jan 29	mid	Nothing to report.	All entries made by J.D. Kenny
		20	One platoon escort transport from LES BREBIS to LOOS. They then dug for 2 hours and came up rations to the front line trenches - under the instructions of the 19th Bn LON. REGT. 2 platoons under and deepen PICCADILLY TRENCH under the instructions of the 2/3rd Field Co. RE.	
	31	mid	3 platoons are engaged in repairing a communication trench in the 19th Bn's sub sector.	

This copy has been checked by me

E.D.Murphy Lt
47th Cyclists
3/5/16

To D.A.G.
3rd Echelon.

In accordance with C.R. No. 140/452, I am forwarding a Copy of War Diary for January.

I have looked thoroughly into this matter, but I am unable to obtain conclusive evidence if this War Diary was dispatched. Our Commanding Officer at the time, is now in England and the orderly room clerk is now with another unit.

G. V. Knox Lt.
Cmdg CYCLIST COMPANY,
47 (LONDON) DIVISION

47

Vol VIII

Confidential

War Diary
of Cyclist Company
47th (London) Division

Period Feby 1st – 29th 15

8 Volume

Army Form C. 2118.

WAR DIARY
or
INTELLIGENCE SUMMARY.
(Erase heading not required.)

Instructions regarding War Diaries and Intelligence Summaries are contained in F. S. Regs., Part II. and the Staff Manual respectively. Title pages will be prepared in manuscript.

Place	Date	Hour	Summary of Events and Information	Remarks and references to Appendices
NORTH MAROC	Feb. 1	6 p.m.	The platoon in the front line trenches is relieved and moves to NORTH MAROC.	9 v.R.H
"	" 2	5.30 p.m.	Two platoons move to LOOS and are engaged in deepening and widening PICCADILLY TRENCH under the instructions of the 2/3rd Field Coy. R.E.	9 v.R.H
"	" 3	5.30 p.m.	ditto	9 v.R.H.H
"	" 4	"	ditto	9 v.R.H
"	" 5	7 p.m.	The company move into Divisional Reserve at LES BREBIS	9 v.R.H
LES BREBIS	" 6		Nothing to report.	9 v.R.H
"	" 7		ditto	9 v.R.H
"	" 8		ditto	9 v.R.H
"	" 9	6 p.m.	Company move from Les BREBIS to SOUTH MAROC and are in SUPPORT for the MAROC SECTOR	9 v.R.H
SOUTH MAROC	" 10		Nothing to report.	9 v.R.H
"	" 11		Company move into Centre Sub-Section and are attached to 17th Bn. LONDON REGT (exact position M.3.0.5.4 to M.9.13.3.4. ref. map Sheet 36 c S.W. scale 1/10,000). 17th Bn. are on company's right and left flanks.	9 v.R.H
Centre Sub-Section	" 12		Nothing to report	9 v.R.H

WAR DIARY or INTELLIGENCE SUMMARY

Army Form C. 2118.

Place	Date	Hour	Summary of Events and Information	Remarks and references to Appendices
CENTRE SUB-SECTION	Feb.13		Nothing to report	J.V.R.25
	" 14		One officer badly wounded whilst out on patrol.	J.V.R.25
	" 15		Company move to BRAQUEMONT and are in G.H.Q reserve. 2 platoons attacked K.E.H move to HURIONVILLE	J.V.R.25
BRAQUEMONT	16		Company move to LABUISSIERE and got their cycles back.	J.V.R.25
LABUSSIERE	17		Company move to HURIONVILLE	J.V.R.25
HURIONVILLE	18		Nothing to report	J.V.R.25
"	" 19		Individual training under platoon commanders.	J.V.R.25
"	" 20		Nothing to report.	J.V.R.25
"	" 21		Combined reconnaissance scheme with KING EDWARDS HORSE	J.V.R.25
"	" 22		1 Platoon in conjunction with 1 troop K.E.H, act as mounted troops to the 142d Bde. in a flank guard scheme.	J.V.R.25
"	" 23		Half the Company shooting on range, remainder Individual training under platoon commanders ditto	J.V.R.25
"	" 24			J.V.R.25
"	" 25		Company training (Intercommunication on parallel roads).	J.V.R.25

Army Form C. 2118.

WAR DIARY
or
INTELLIGENCE SUMMARY.

(Erase heading not required.)

Instructions regarding War Diaries and Intelligence Summaries are contained in F.S. Regs., Part II. and the Staff Manual respectively. Title pages will be prepared in manuscript.

Place	Date	Hour	Summary of Events and Information	Remarks and references to Appendices
HURIONVILLE	Feb 26		Company training (concentration march).	9.v.r.17.25
"	" 27		Nothing to report.	9.v.r.25
"	" 28		Combined scheme with K.E.H. (advance guard work).	9.v.r.25
"	" 29		Individual training under platoon commanders.	9.v.r.26

Thos S Harrison Lt
(Owg 9 CYCLIST COMPANY,
47th (LONDON) DIVISION.)

Vol IX

49)

Confidential

War Diary
of
Cyclist Company
47th (London) Division

Series March 1st — 31st.

Volume X

Army Form C. 2118.

WAR DIARY
or
INTELLIGENCE SUMMARY.
(Erase heading not required.)

Place	Date	Hour	Summary of Events and Information	Remarks and references to Appendices
HUIONVILLE	March 1		Field Day with K.E.H.	2/Lt J. Polverley 2nd Lt
	Mar. 2		Drill A.M. Lecture P.M.	
	" 3		Nothing to report. Drill/drill	"
	" 4		" "	"
	" 5		Church Parade at 10.30 A.M. Lecture by Major Homer to Officers & N.C.Os of B.M.T.	"
	" 6		Nothing to report.	"
	" 7		March to MARTHES at 12 noon with K.E.H.	"
MARTHES	Mar. 8		Nothing to report.	
	" 9		Advance Guard scheme by bicycle only.	
	" 10		March to BRUAY.	
BRUAY	" 11		Nothing to report.	
	" 12		ditto	J.V.K.ZL
	" 13		Individual Training by Platoon commanders (Advance guard scheme)	J.V.K.ZL
	" 14		ditto	J.V.K.ZL
	" 15		4 Platoons under the O.C. Company move to VILLERS-AU-BOIS and are attached to the 141st Bde. for tactical purposes. 2 platoons and H.Q's move to MAGNICOURT-LE-COMTE and are attached to J.V.K.ZL

WAR DIARY
or
INTELLIGENCE SUMMARY.

Army Form C. 2118.

Place	Date	Hour	Summary of Events and Information	Remarks and references to Appendices
MAGNICOURT	Mar.16		Four platoons with 141st. Brigade in trenches ½ mile S.E. of SOUCHEZ. H.Q. + 2 platoons at MAGNICOURT. Lest Lt Critchley-Smith.	
"	" 17		Nothing to report	ditto
"	" 18		"	"
"	" 19		"	"
"	" 20		One N.C.O. killed + five others wounded in trenches ½ mile S.E. of SOUCHEZ. (One wounded since dead.)	"
"	" 21		Four platoons with 141st Brigade relieved and spent night at VILLERS-au-BOIS.	"
HERMIN	" 22		H.Q. established and four platoons at HERMIN. One platoon goes to hut ¼ mile E of CARENCY on Bois de Borigny.	"
"	"		CARENCY-SOUCHEZ road. One platoon to hut in Bois de Borigny.	"
"	" 23		Nothing to report. ditto	"
"	" 24		Bois de Borigny platoon joins platoon at ¼ E of CARENCY on CARENCY-SOUCHEZ road.	"
"	" 25		Nothing to report. ditto	"
"	" 26		"	"
"	" 27		"	"
"	" 28		"	Lt Critchley-Smith
"	" 29		Two platoons E of CARENCY relieved by 2 platoons from HERMIN	"
"	30		Nothing to report	

Army Form C. 2118.

WAR DIARY
or
INTELLIGENCE SUMMARY.
(Erase heading not required.)

Instructions regarding War Diaries and Intelligence Summaries are contained in F. S. Regs., Part II. and the Staff Manual respectively. Title pages will be prepared in manuscript.

Place	Date	Hour	Summary of Events and Information	Remarks and references to Appendices
HERMIN	March 30		Nothing to report	H Murphy 2=Lt.
"	" 31		" " "	"
"	April 1		" " "	"
"	" 2			

Thos H Harrison Lt
Comdg.
CYCLIST COMPANY.
47[?] LONDON DIVISION.

1577 Wt.W10791/1773 500,000 1/15 D. D. & L. A.D.S.S./Forms/C. 2118.

Confidential

War Diary
of the Cyclist Company
47th (London) Division

For the month of April 1916.

Vol X

Army Form C. 2118.

CYCLIST COMPANY,

47th (LONDON) DIVISION.

WAR DIARY
or
INTELLIGENCE SUMMARY.

(Erase heading not required.)

Instructions regarding War Diaries and Intelligence Summaries are contained in F. S. Regs., Part II and the Staff Manual respectively. Title pages will be prepared in manuscript.

Place	Date	Hour	Summary of Events and Information	Remarks and references to Appendices
HERMIN	April 1		Communication Trench Party (strength 1 N.C.O., 1 officer and 2 platoons) work by day in CABARET ROUGE Trench. Communication Trench Party in the Bois de Bouvigny (strength 1 officer and 1 platoon) work by night at a disused trench running from X.11.B.7.7 to church at ABLAIN-ST-NAZAIRE.	9. v.R.21.
	" 2		ditto	9. v.R.21.
	" 3		ditto	9. v.R.21.
	" 4		ditto	9. v.R.21.
	" 5		Communication Trench Parties are relieved by the 3 platoons in HERMIN. Some work as before	9. v.R.21.
	" 6		Nothing to Report	9. v.R.21.
	" 7		ditto	9. v.R.21.
	" 8		ditto	9. v.R.21.
	" 9		The maintenance of the CABARET ROUGE TRENCH is taken over by the 46th DIVISIONAL CYCLIST COMPANY so the COMMUNICATION TRENCH PARTY start work on the ERSATZ TRENCH (between the CABARET ROUGE and the ZOUAVE VALLEY) A reinforcement of 6 men arrives.	9. v.R.21.
	" 10		Nothing to Report.	9. v.R.21.
	" 11		ditto	9. v.R.21.
	" 12		The weekly inter-relief takes place (see above).	9. v.R.21.

Army Form C. 2118.

CYCLIST COMPANY.
(7) LONDON DIVISION.

WAR DIARY
or
INTELLIGENCE SUMMARY.
(Erase heading not required.)

Instructions regarding War Diaries and Intelligence
Summaries are contained in F. S. Regs., Part II.
and the Staff Manual respectively. Title pages
will be prepared in manuscript.

Place	Date	Hour	Summary of Events and Information	Remarks and references to Appendices
HERMIN	April 13		Nothing to Report	J.V.R.H
"	14		ditto	J.V.R.25
"	15		ditto	J.V.R.25
"	16		ditto	J.V.R.25
"	17		ditto	J.V.R.25
"	18		A Reinforcement of 2 officers arrived.	J.V.R.25
"	19		The weekly inter-relief takes place. 2 platoons near CARENCY work on 130 trench between CABARET ROUGE and Bn. H.Q's CENTRE SUB-SECTION.	J.V.R.25
"	20		Nothing to Report	J.V.R.25
"	21		ditto	J.V.R.25
"	22		ditto	J.V.R.25
"	23		ditto	J.V.R.25
"	24		ditto A reinforcement of 6 men arrives	J.V.R.25
"	25		One of the platoons at HERMIN, and one officer joins the party in the dug-outs near CARENCY, and works on the CABARET ROAD TRENCH from X 23 A 5-0 towards VILLERS-AU-BOIS	J.V.R.25
"	26		Two of the platoons near CARENCY are relieved. One of these platoons goes to VILLERS-AU-BOIS, and works on CABARET ROAD TRENCH from X 23 A 5-0 towards VILLERS-AU-BOIS; the other returns to	J.V.R.25

Army Form C. 2118.

WAR DIARY
or
INTELLIGENCE SUMMARY.
(Erase heading not required.)

Instructions regarding War Diaries and Intelligence Summaries are contained in F. S. Regs., Part II. and the Staff Manual respectively. Title pages will be prepared in manuscript.

Place	Date	Hour	Summary of Events and Information	Remarks and references to Appendices
HERMIN	April 26		to HERMIN, the three platoons in dug-outs near CARENCY all work on 130 trench (see above).	J v KSt
"	" 27		Nothing to report.	J v K St
"	" 28		O.C. COMPANY goes to VILLERS-AU-BOIS to take over command of the 5 platoons in VILLERS-AU-BOIS, in the dug-outs near CARENCY, and in the BOIS DE BOUVIGNY.	J v K St
"	" 29		Nothing to Report.	J v K St
"	" 30		The platoon at BOUVIGNY is relieved. A reinforcement of 8 men arrives.	J v K St

J v Kraat Lt
o.c. of CYCLIST COMPANY,
(47 LONDON DIVISION.)

War Diary
of the
Cyclist Company
Hqrs London Division

for the month of May 1916.

Army Form C. 2118.

CYCLIST COMPANY.
(2nd) (LONDON) DIVISION.

WAR DIARY
or
INTELLIGENCE SUMMARY
(Erase heading not required.)

Instructions regarding War Diaries and Intelligence Summaries are contained in F.S. Regs., Part II. and the Staff Manual respectively. Title pages will be prepared in manuscript.

Place	Date	Hour	Summary of Events and Information	Remarks and references to Appendices
HERMIN	May 1st		One Officer leaves to join R.F.C.	SR
HERMIN	2nd		O.C. Coy VILLERS AU BOIS. 1 Platoon at VILLERS AU BOIS. 3 Platoons in Dugouts near CARENCY, 1 in BOIS DE BOUVIGNY all on trench maintenance.	SR
HERMIN	3rd		ditto	SR
HERMIN	4th		ditto	SR
HERMIN	5th		ditto	SR
HERMIN	6th		All four platoons return to HERMIN and leave the line. Company H.Q. at HERMIN	SR
HERMIN	7th		Returning to Report	SR
HERMIN	8th		ditto	SR
HERMIN	9th		ditto	SR
VINCLY	10th		One Officer returns to 18th London Regt. Cyclist Company and K.E.H. (47th A.D.M.T.) proceed via VINCLY to join the 1st Cavalry Division for training.	SR
ECAMES	11th		Company H.Q. Chateau FLORINETHUN. ECAMES (6 miles W. of SAMER Ref. Map. CALAIS 13) Attached to 1st Cavalry Division for training. H.Q. of Divisional Mounted Troops School HESDIN L'ABBÉ	SR

Army Form C. 2118.

CYCLIST COMPANY,
47. (LONDON) DIVISION.

WAR DIARY
or
INTELLIGENCE SUMMARY.
(Erase heading not required.)

Instructions regarding War Diaries and Intelligence Summaries are contained in F. S. Regs., Part II. and the Staff Manual respectively. Title pages will be prepared in manuscript.

Place	Date 1916	Hour	Summary of Events and Information	Remarks and references to Appendices
ECAMES	May 12th		Nothing to Report	A.1.
ECAMES	13th		Nothing to Report	A.1
ECAMES	14th		Nothing to Report	A1
ECAMES	15th		Training commences. Lectures on "Reconnaissance and Patrolling" & "Map Reading"	
ECAMES	16th		3 Platoons "Wood Fighting". 3 Platoons scheme for Independent Mission. Lecture "Protection"	
ECAMES	17th		Lectures "Messages"	A.1
ECAMES	18th		Lecture "Field Sketching"	A1
ECAMES	19th		Scheme with 1st and 2nd Cavalry Brigades. Holding a weakly entrenched position.	A1
ECAMES	20th		Scheme "Protection of Billets"	A1
ECAMES	21st		Nothing to Report	A1
ECAMES	22nd		Scheme "Advanced and Rear Guards"	A1
ECAMES	23rd		Seventy Eight (78) Men and N.C.Os return to 47th Division to form various units owing to an order reducing the establishment of Cyclist companies and transferring them from the Division to the Corps. New Establishment One Captain and three Subalterns and Ninety-five Other Ranks. (4 Officers and 95 O.Rs.) Lecture "Messages" and "Artillery in Open Warfare".	A1omal

1577 Wt.W10791/1773 500,000 1/15 D.D. & L. A.D.S.S./Forms/C. 2118.

Army Form C. 2118.

WAR DIARY
or
INTELLIGENCE SUMMARY.

(Erase heading not required.)

CYCLIST COMPANY,
47 (LONDON) DIVISION.

Instructions regarding War Diaries and Intelligence Summaries are contained in F. S. Regs., Part II and the Staff Manual respectively. Title pages will be prepared in manuscript.

Place	Date 1916	Hour	Summary of Events and Information	Remarks and references to Appendices
	MAY			
ECAMES	24th		Scheme with 1st & 49th Cavalry Brigades. Attacking and cutting off Rearguards from Yetting.	A.P.
ECAMES	25th		Took into an entrenched position. Scheme night 25th/26th. "Night Concentration March and taking up tactical position at Suver."	A.P.
ECAMES	26th		"Attack upon small landing force of mounted troops." Nothing to report	A.P.
ECAMES	27th		Scheme	A.P.
ECAMES	28th		Nothing to report	A.P.
ECAMES	29th			A.P.
VINCLY	30th		Proceeded as a Company to VINCLY (HAZEBROUCK. 5A of map) en route to join the IV Corps Cyclist Bn. as "C" Company.	A.P.
Mt ST ELOY	31st		The 47th Cyclist Company join the IV Corps Cyclist Bn. as "C" Company at Mt ST ELOY (LENS 11 inf. map.)	A.P.

Thos H Harrison
Cpl.

CYCLIST COMPANY,
47 (LONDON) DIVISION.

1577 Wt.W10791/1773 500,000 1/15 D. D. & L. A.D.S.S./Forms/C. 2118.

War Diary
of the
Cyclist Company
47th (London) Division
for the month of
June 1916

Army Form C. 2118.

WAR DIARY
or
INTELLIGENCE SUMMARY.
(Erase heading not required.)

47th Divisional Cyclist Co.
("C" Coy 4th Corps Cyclist Bn.)

Place	Date	Hour	Summary of Events and Information	Remarks and references to Appendices
BOIS DES ALLEUX Mt ST ELOY (Map Ref) FRANCE Sht 51c 1st Edn. 1/40,000	1.6.16		Whole Company joined IV Corps Cyclist Battalion (less men attached to 47th Division as Infantry in order to reduce the strength of the Company to 4 Officers 96 O.R.s plus men attached to H.Q. 4th Corps Cyclist Bn.)	J.S.May 5/t
	2.6.16 to 7.6.16		"C" Company employed on Trench boarding for 2nd Division (1st E. Anglian R.E.) between CARENCY and HOSPITAL CORNER in BAVIERE RD Trench. (Ref. Sht 36 c Edn. 6 1/40,000)	
	8.6.16 to 14.6.16		20 Men on Fatigue Duty at HOSPITAL CORNER. Rest working on BAVIERE RD. Both men on Fatigue Duty and on Trench BOARDING did 6 hrs daily 9 A.M. to 3 P.M.	
	15.6.16 16.6.16		Whole Company go on fnt. of Repairing dugouts at HOSPITAL CORNER (SOUCHEZ — CARENCY RD. ½ mile E. of CARENCY) working in three shifts of 20 men each doing 6 hrs in 24 skull per day. (N.B. Clock time advanced 1hr. on 14th inst. 11°° P.M. becoming MIDNIGHT.)	

Army Form C. 2118.

WAR DIARY
or
INTELLIGENCE SUMMARY.
(Erase heading not required.)

47th Divisional Cyclist Co
("C" Coy. IV Corps Cyclist Bn.)

Place	Date	Hour	Summary of Events and Information	Remarks and references to Appendices
TANGRY	17-6-16		Company now with IV Corps Cyclist Bn. to TANGRY via ACQ, AUBIGNY, LA BELLE EPINE, MARQUAY, BRYAS, and VALHUON (Map ref LENS 11 1/100,000)	
(MAP ref) LENS 11 1/100,000	18-6-16		Battalion Training	
	19-6-16		Scheme with CORPS MOUNTED TROOPS (Rear Guard) under Col HERMAN.	
	20-6-16		Officer, Supernumerary to establishment, Capt LESTER of 3rd/2nd LONDON DIV. CYCLIST Co arrived for duty.	
	21-6-16		Battalion Training	
	22-6-16		Battalion Training	
	23-6-16		Scheme with Corps Mtd. Troops (Advd. Guard)	
	24-6-16		Battalion Training	
	29-6-16		One Officer and 12 O.R. from B & A Coys report to 4 Cohs A.R.M. for duty on Tramming Posts on line HERSIN — LES QUATRE VENTS 28 O.R. with LENS 11 1/100,000	
			Battalion Training Scheme with Corps Mounted Troops (Adv. Guard)	

Thos N Harvey Capt
CYCLIST COMPANY,
47 (LONDON) DIVISION.

Vol/2

War Diary.
of the
Cyclist Company
47th (London) Division.
for the month of July 1916.

WAR DIARY or INTELLIGENCE SUMMARY

Army Form C. 2118.

47th Div. Cyc. Co. ("C" Coy IV Corps Cyc. Bn)

Place	Date	Hour	Summary of Events and Information	Remarks and references to Appendices
TANGRY	1.7.16		Training continued.	
	2.7.16		Constructional work continued on 200yd. Range at 622 C 3,3. FRANCE Sheet 36 B 3rd Edition.	
	3.7.16 to 7.7.16		Training with Battalion.	
	8.7.16		Training. One reinforcement from 47th Div. Base Depôt HAVRE.	
	9.7.16 to 11.7.16		Musketry	
ERNY	12.7.16		March to ERNY S.t JULIEN via FIEFS, FEBVIN PALFART, FLECHIN, and CUHEM. New camp pitched. (Inch n.t. HAZEBROUCK 5A 1/100,000)	
S.t JULIEN			Training. Two reinforcements arrived from 47th Div. Base Depôt HAVRE.	
HAZ. 5A.	13.7.16		Training with IV Corps Cavalry.	
	14.7.16 to 18.7.16		Training with IV Corps Battalion.	
	19.7.16		(47th Cyc) "C" Company men return from 2nd Div. H.Q. for duty with IV Corps Battalion.	Sig./1/N.M.T. 7th Div. Cyc. Co. 13th 47th Div. Cyc Co. IV Corps

WAR DIARY
or
INTELLIGENCE SUMMARY.

Army Form C. 2118.

47th Div. Cyc. Co. ("C" Coy IV Corps. Cyc. Bn)

Place	Date	Hour	Summary of Events and Information	Remarks and references to Appendices
ERNY St JULIEN	20.7.16 to 24.7.16		Training with IV Corps Cavalry Regiment.	
OLHAIN	25.7.16		Moved to OLHAIN (nr HOUDAIN) via FIEFS, PERNES, CAMBLAIN-CHATELAIN, DIVION, HOUDAIN and REBREUVE. (Map reference LENS 11/100,000)	
BOIS de VERDREL	26.7.16		Bn. H.Q. remain at OLHAIN. "B" Coy to BOIS de VERDREL and "C" Coy (47th Div. Cyclist) move with 3 Platoons and take over from "D" Coy H.A.C.. Work commenced at night on E. extremity of NOTRE DAME de LORETTE under IV Corps Signals. Bury cable 6 feet deep, fill in, and fill up to 2 feet above ground level. Cable for communication purposes from O.P.s to Battery positions.	
	28.7.16		"C" Coy (47 Div. Cyc. Co.) men return from 47th Signals and A.P.M. 47th Divn. Work as usual every night on NOTRE DAME.	
	29.7.16			
	30.7.16 to 31.7.16		Work as usual bringing cable. Eleven cables buried, each cable containing 4 wires.	

Lloyd Harris Capt.
Cmdg. Cyclist Company
47th (London) Division

G. Mercliff
(47) 4 Div Cyc Co.
IV corps Cyc Br

www.ingramcontent.com/pod-product-compliance
Lightning Source LLC
Chambersburg PA
CBHW081239170426
43191CB00034B/1984